Mommy & Daddy ♥ Me 2 Much

Self-Esteem—Love Yourself; Don't Hurt Yourself

Illustrations by Violeta Honasan

Copyright © 2013 by Rolanda Russell. 121906-BROO
ISBN: Softcover 978-1-4797-6438-9
Ebook 978-1-4797-6439-6

All rights reserved. No part of this book may be reproduced or transmitted
in any form or by any means, electronic or mechanical, including photocopying, recording,
or by any information storage and retrieval system, without permission
in writing from the copyright owner.

Rev. Date: 02/26/2013

To order additional copies of this book, contact:
Xlibris Corporation
1-888-795-4274
www.Xlibris.com
Orders@Xlibris.com

About me......

Hi, my name is Crissy, and I am six years old going on thirty-six because my mommy and daddy taught me so many things. I have three brothers, a mommy, and a daddy, and I will tell you all the things they taught me because of how much they love me too much.

Born this way.....

My mommy and daddy told me that when they were young and in school, just like I am today, kids made fun of them and sometimes even called them not-so-nice names. They told me that this happened to almost every adult when they were growing up and that it is just how kids are and that it is not right, but that is how they are.

They told me that if every parent in this world would tell their own story to their children, it may help their child to have a better understanding of how to deal with it when it is happening to them and that it is never ever the end of the world and no one should hurt themselves. Don't do it.

My mommy and daddy said that parents should always instill positive thoughts in their children and always compliment them about any and everything often enough.

My mommy and daddy told me it is important that we have a good relationship with each other from the ground up, that way we can talk about any and everything especially the most difficult ones. They said that there will be ups and downs, difficult times of life, and that that is just how life is, but children should never ever keep the most difficult issues they are facing from their parents. Whatever it is, parents, teachers, and authorities are there to help.

God Loves Us All

My mommy and daddy told me that God made me along with everyone else in his own image; the way he likes and wants us to be.

We don't have to be the same color, size, or height, but we are perfect and beautiful in his eyes and should be in everyone else's eyes.

We must love who we are because that is how God loves us and wants us to be. If we don't love ourselves, it will be impossible to love others, and hatred will be on its way into our hearts.

If God can give his only son, Jesus Christ, to save us (John 3:16), who are we to dislike anyone?

Never Make Fun

They taught us we should never make fun of people no matter how they look; the world would be dull and boring if we all looked the same. Being comfortable about who you are and accepting others for who they are is the best thing you can do for yourself and the rest of the world. There would be less hatred as well.

We are born into our own ethnicity (race) because that is where God, and only God, wants us to be, whether we like it or not. We should like it because God always knows what's best. We may not like the food or the dressing of some ethnic groups, but always keep in your mind that it is God's way and not yours.

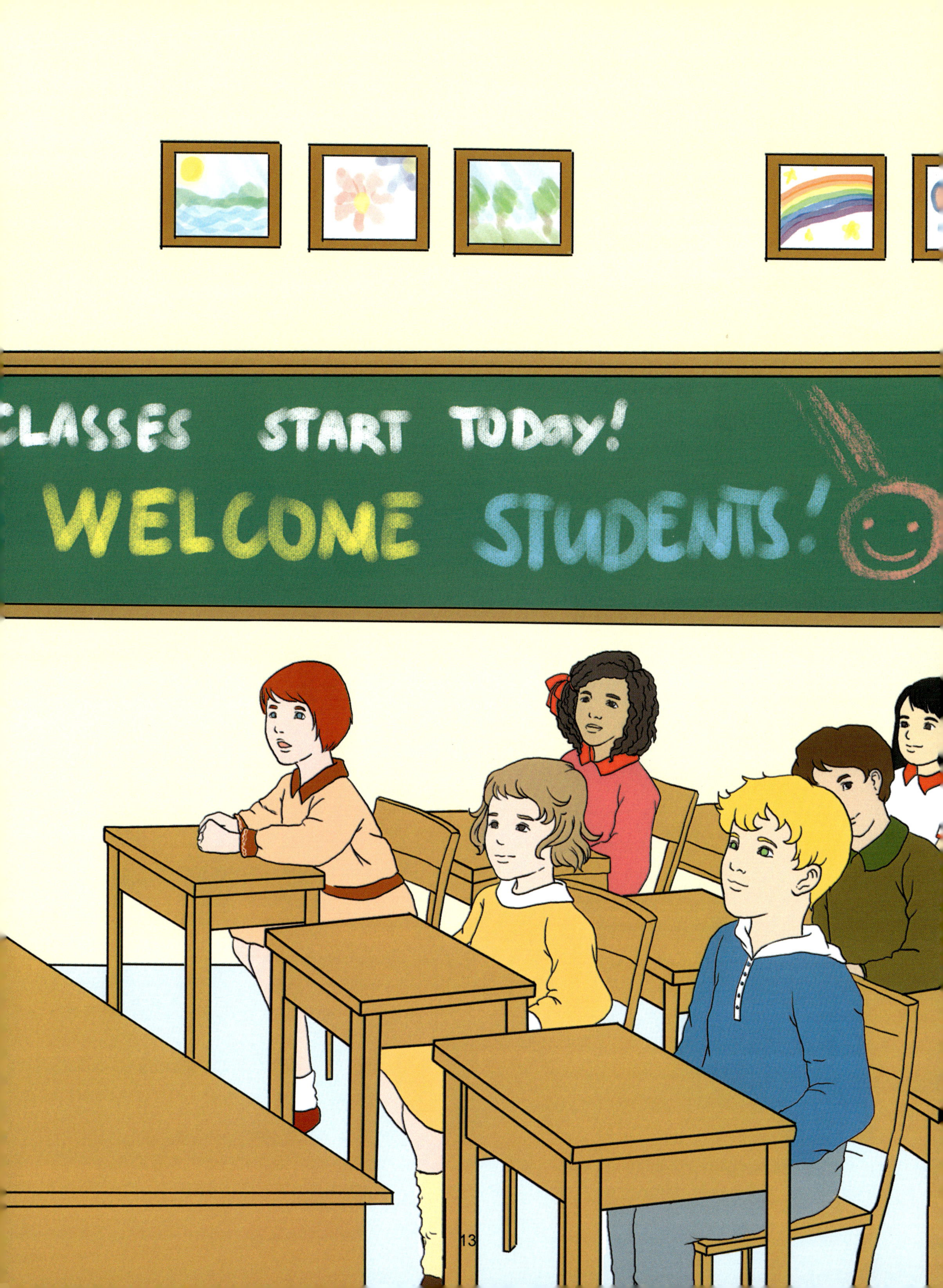
CLASSES START TODay!
WELCOME STUDENTS!

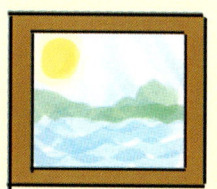

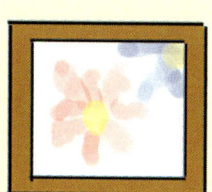

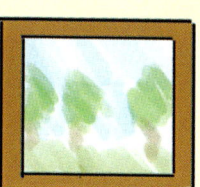

Tell Your Parents/Someone

If someone makes fun of you because of how you look, always tell your mommy, daddy, or the teacher if you are at school. If it's someone in your neighborhood and your mommy and daddy knows them, they may go over and talk to their parents. It should never be ignored. It solves absolutely nothing to hurt yourself, so just don't do it.

They told us we all have uniqueness about ourselves, things that we like or like to do, and not everyone will like it, but that's what makes us even more special.

A Story

My daddy took my brother and me to the doctor for our regular checkup, and the doctor told my dad that we are going to be as tall as our mommy. I told my mommy when I got home, and she said, "Tall and beautiful"—"handsome" for my brother. We can't wait because we love her so much.

I always thought my mom was older than my dad because she is taller, so funny, but now I know that short people can be older than tall people.

Something Nice to Say—Say Nothing

My mommy and daddy said it is not polite (nice) to stare at someone; it is rude. If you have a compliment (something nice) to say to someone, just say it and move on, or if you don't have something nice to say, say nothing.

Confidence vs. Rudeness: Another Story

My mom remembered a long time ago when she was trying to discipline my older brother on the telephone when he was a little, little boy, and out of nowhere he said to her, "Do you want me to hang up the phone on you?" That was the first time her sweet little angel ever said anything to her that was so surprising, and though she couldn't laugh until she finished speaking to him, she had to laugh; she recalled she was so shocked.

She said that, looking back on it now, it was a sure sign of confidence coming from her sweet little angel at the time. He must have been two and a half or three years old.

Just Like the Trees

Just like the trees needs sunshine and water to grow, so do we. Discipline should not be a sign of abuse. The trees are often rocked back and forth by strong winds and heavy rain, yet they manage to grow solid and straight. We need to be trained from the ground up and not from up go down, like our grandparents did for our parents and our parents for us. My older brother today is very confident and positive about life, and I love him.

The Green Screen (People on TV and in Magazines)

My mommy and daddy said the people we see on TV and in magazines are all put together to look that way to do their jobs, just like doctors, nurses, and judges have to dress with their outfits to do their jobs. No one is born to look that good all the time, and people shouldn't think that or do anything that would harm themselves to look like them. There are also lots of camera tricks to make them look like that. It can make them look like any size they want: skinny, fat, short, or tall, and even as if they have perfect skin. It is all the tricks of the camera.

Love Yourself

My mommy and daddy taught me that if we don't have anything nice to say to someone, don't say anything. Keep the mouth shut.

The best thing of all is that I love myself and dislike no one because of how they look.

I will always remember to love myself; don't hurt myself, because . . .

This is how my mommy and daddy loves me too much.

Empowerment

My contribution to you by helping to empower you through self esteem, to walk confidently with your head held high and to know that you are loved and have every right to be here

Other book

My contribution to help protect you from bullies as in my other book "S.T.O.P. Bully" to not tolerate bullies by telling someone when you feel you are being bullied.

Edwards Brothers Malloy
Thorofare, NJ USA
August 8, 2014